THANKS
FOR THE
MOUNTAIN

THANKS FOR THE MOUNTAIN

Erling and Marge Wold

AUGSBURG PUBLISHING HOUSE
Minneapolis, Minnesota

Contents

Prolog

ERLING:

On that sparkling August day when a wave dashed me against the ocean floor, breaking my neck and totally paralyzing me, I entered into an ecstatic experience of God's presence and grace. Marge and I look back on those hospital months as one of the most joy-filled times in our life together. We praised God for each day and for every returning bodily function as I learned to move and finally to walk again.

It is this joy and praise that we tried to share in our first book, *What Do I Have to Do—Break My Neck?*

About four months after the accident other emotions slowly came into focus: depression, doubt, despair. They came in the wake of the knowledge that I would never again be physically what I had been before. I caught myself wishing I had died on the beach.

Immense waves of despair rolled over me, bringing a new brokenness and paralysis of the spirit—a suffering more intense than any I had known physically. The

9

beauty of that Minnesota winter was lost to me, and I only knew that my feelings found their counterpart in the frozen landscape.

Then on a Thursday early in April, I picked up the morning paper from the threshold of our apartment door and read a news story that spoke a special word to me. It was the story of Bonnie Cutsforth of Rice Lake, Wisconsin, who had just died at sixteen years of age, a victim of bone cancer.

The Minneapolis Tribune carried her story under the headline, CANCER OR NOT, BONNIE CLIMBED HER MOUNTAIN. Stricken at 14 years of age, Bonnie understood the nature of her illness and talked freely about how long she had to live. She confided to a high school counselor that there was one thing she longed to do before she died. Bonnie wanted to see the mountains in Colorado and visit her brother who was in the army and stationed in Colorado Springs.

After all the medical expenses there was no family money for such a trip. Her counselor told some of the other teachers at the high school, who passed the word on to a few students. That's how a fund was started which eventually sent Bonnie and her folks to Colorado. Without publicity the word spread from the school to other sections of the community until there were many contributors.

Bonnie had never been on a long trip or ridden in an airplane or seen a mountain. The newspaper quoted her mother as saying, "She was really thrilled. She waded in a cold mountain stream and was up early every morning. Then she decided to climb this large mountain. We were scared as we watched her climb. We begged her to turn around and come down. But she said she was going to do it. It was amazing how she could climb. And she made it."

Six months later Bonnie died. But before her death she wrote a little note to the students at Rice Lake High School: "Hey, thanks for the mountain."

Bonnie's story became a parable of suffering, since Bonnie had really been climbing two mountains, the one of rock and soil and brush and the other of pain and agony and weakness.

The mountain of my own disability and despair loomed large before me when I read of Bonnie.

This book is the story of my struggle up its slopes and how Marge and I are learning to say, "Hey God, thanks for the mountain!"

We're climbing it together.

The
Mountain

ERLING:

After my neck was broken, I woke each morning faced with the necessity of doing battle with my own personal "mountain."

At night I would fall asleep hugging to myself a secret longing that in the morning the mountain would have disappeared and my body would have been restored to its pre-accident vitality.

But in the morning, it was always there.

It's still there.

The mountain is my physical disability which stands as an ever-present barrier between me and all of the joyous and productive living my heart longs for and which I must have to experience any sense of my own identity. Realizing this goal in my daily living involves me in a day-by-day struggle to reach the summit of that rugged obstacle blocking my way.

This is the shape of my mountain:

I waken early every morning. Never a late sleeper, I sometimes wish now that I could sleep a little longer and postpone the moment of movement. I lie quietly for awhile after consciousness comes, recalling Bible verses and focusing on thoughts of praise. Inevitably, the time comes to move, to get going. My mountain begins to form.

As I make the first in the series of conscious muscle motions it takes to get out of bed, my entire body quivers as it fights against activity. Life's juices seem to flow down out of my face and upper torso, draining my will of all of its energy. Agonizing effort is required for every movement as I force arms and legs to stretch their reluctant muscles. At least five times more energy is now involved in moving at all. Invisible sandbags drag at my joints and lie heavily cocooned around my body. Paralysis compresses my chest like the hands of a malevolent giant, and I fight to get enough life-sustaining air.

Fantasies begin to dance in my brain as the struggle with rebellious muscles and ligaments continues. I remember the former days when I arose early and donned casual attire and tennis shoes in preparation for a morning jog of one or two miles. I recall the brush of fresh morning air against my face as I ran, the good feeling of damp earth underfoot, the sense of well-being as muscles moved in harmony with an easy jogging gait, the fulfilling return to home and family and a warm shower and breakfast. *What a way to start the day,* I often thought, as I went on to the daily routine of my pastoral ministry.

A harsh return to reality overwhelms me.

16

"God, help me!" I cry, just as the mountain of my pain seems about to crush me.

The echo of my own cries returns, amplified by an entire mountain range of needs that appear next to my own. I think then of all the persons I know who, like me, waken to a daily struggle with their own personal mountains of need—those conditions or burdens which prevent them from experiencing joy and praise.

For instance, ancient skeletons reveal the centuries of suffering of untold millions who have lived with the never-ending pain of arthritis. I am aware that compared to the burdens of others my disability appears as a mere foothill up against the awesome mass of Mount Everest!

What strange shapes and proportions the entire catalog of human burdens assumes! Birth deformities which set one apart from others; crippling dependencies on alcohol, on other drugs and on people around us; the wounded who lie in hospitals because they answered the call to fight in the wars of the world; the young who have lost limbs in motorcycle and automobile accidents; the blind and the deaf; the one person out of three who discovers dread cancer in their bodies; all of the unknown strugglers with hidden fears and despairs.

My first frightening encounter with the fears that lurk about my mountain came some months after my accident. The hospital experience was sheer ecstasy; God's special measure of grace which floods in to support one in crisis surrounded me with joy and gave rise to bubbling praise! Even the total paralysis which I experienced at that time produced no anxiety or panic in me. The weeks afterwards when therapy continued to bring a return to movement filled me with enthusiasm and confidence.

Then the day came when I openly faced the question that had been tugging at the edges of my consciousness but which I had refused to recognize before, "Will I ever really be well again?"

Other questions poured quickly through this opening wedge.

"What will my future be?

"Will Marge always have to work to support me?

"What if I am hurt in another accident?

"What if arthritis sets in?

"Will my hands always be stiff?

"Will I ever be able to type again?

"What if I should become ill and unable to exercise every day?

"How soon would encroaching stiffness send me back into total paralysis?

"How much will the natural infirmities of age aggravate my condition?"

These questions triggered the anxieties that crouched in the shadows of my mind. I began to experience moments of depression and despair. Then I walked with Luther, who said that everyone must face God without a proxy. In the deepest physical battles of time, we cannot ignore the fact that the struggle is essentially a spiritual one, and the temptation to feel forsaken by God and people becomes a part of everyday living. So all of us are tempted to be anxious, to settle into the quicksand of depression. We know the fragmentation of time, its disillusionment, the confusion that surrounds us, the

18

corruption, the fear, mistrust, the injustice of our own condition and the uncaring lack of concern we seem to see in others.

I brooded about my impaired physique and my disabled appearance. I suspected that people were looking at my immobile hands and remarking upon my jerky, unstable gait. *I've really aged,* I thought, studying my appearance in the unsympathetic mirror. A deepening sense of unworthiness made me vulnerable and magnified even the smallest hurt into depression. *How can my wife love me?* I brooded. We used to play tennis, ride bikes, swim. Self-pity nagged at me, and I succumbed to periods of dark moodiness. My nerves were on edge, and the smallest real or imagined slight upset me.

I even reacted negatively to the cheerfulness of others.

Not only did my physical condition bother me, but I began to wonder if my ability to think had been affected by the blow to my head on the ocean floor. Because my activity was drastically reduced, hours of tedium dragged on.

I lost interest in everything except my body. To concentrate on anything else meant fighting through the distractions of strange physical sensations: tingling nerves, prickling skin, numbness, a crushing heaviness on shoulders and chest as I sat, the leaden weight of my feet when I stood or walked, the constant stiffness of my fingers.

The exhilaration of my death/resurrection experience with its built-in opportunities for witness, the supremely heightened communication channel to God throughout my hospitalization, the extended concern of both hospital staff and family during the anxious hours following my rescue from an ocean grave—all slipped away in the lonely struggle to adjust to a radically changed lifestyle.

The answer to my question, "Will I ever really be well again?" came with crushing certainty. *I will never again know what's it's like to be free of physical disability!*

I reached out for God. He was suddenly remote.

Only the mountain was near, and in the valley below I despaired.

"Why did you spare my life? Why didn't you let me die in the ocean?"

All of us who are concerned with both mental and spiritual health know without question that depression is the deadly smog that is smothering so many people. It's the new epidemic, universal as the common cold. It's been called the "epidemic of the '70s." Despair and hopelessness depress the lives of some eight million Americans.

Even the young—stereotyped as "carefree"—are not immune to the ravages of depression. Among those eight million victims are an increasing number of young people. Although students now are generally more affluent than their predecessors, have a wider range of subjects to explore, have more freedom to gratify all their desires, and have more opportunities to travel, depression grips so many. The ultimate, visible sign of despair is death by suicide. Researchers estimate that more than 20,000 young people between the ages of 15 and 24 will be attempting suicide in the next twelve months and that about 4000 of them will succeed. Death by suicide is also rising at an alarming rate in communities for the aged.

What causes these pressed-down feelings? What is it that buries one in his own dark juices? What paralyzes one's will so that all reason for continuing to live drains away? What makes the dark shadows of the night stay to darken the daylight hours?

It's possible to be capable of analyzing our depressions, of dissecting them, and putting them under the microscope of our intellect and of our faith and still not be able to cope with them emotionally. That's because the hard inner core of depression is *helplessness*. I arrived at that point when I realized that there was nothing I could do to change my condition or to restore myself to my former wholeness.

I felt as cornered as the helicopter pilot I met only months after my injury. A bullet had entered his leg while he was flying over Vietnam. It plunged through his torso and out his back, severing his spinal cord. I saw him as a mirror of my own helplessness as he sat in his wheelchair, permanently immobilized from the waist down. He had so much going for him—brilliance, training, a beautifully supportive family, a wife who visibly cared. But he knew, as I did, that a single foreboding reality hung over him. He would never walk again.

There is a naked realism to helplessness. There is no way you can pull yourself up by your own bootstraps to change your own condition. You are caught in a corner, and there seems to be no way out. The comedian Fred Allen used to quip, "Run to the roundhouse, Nellie, they can't corner you there!" But you see no humor anywhere, and there is no roundhouse in which to hide. You are exposed, vulnerable, nakedly helpless.

That is the shape of the mountain.

Once defined, what does one do about it?

Basically, two alternatives present themselves. One is *to reject the mountain as reality!* the other is *to rejoice in the mountain as ultimate reality!*

If you choose the first alternative and reject the reality of your situation, then your behavior may assume one or another of the following forms.

The pretense says the mountain isn't there. Now no one consciously makes a statement as obviously unrealistic as this, "If I ignore it, it'll go away," But I'm well aware that sometimes I've acted that way. I deliberately lose myself in whatever work I'm doing; I read every magazine and book that comes my way in order to avoid thinking; I try hard to avoid situations where my "difference" is apparent.

I could easily have gone the drug route to escape from reality in the early stages of my recovery. My muscles are frequently gripped by uncontrollable tremors. Too much exercise or too little exercise produce the same shaking reaction. I often feel cold all over my body even in the warmest weather. In the hospital I was given a powerful sedative three times a day to control the teeth-chattering tremors and shakings. When I was released from the hospital, the pills went home wtih me. I found myself looking forward to the tranquility and release from bodily sensations which they gave me. Sleep came more easily and I welcomed this drugged escape into quiet rest.

22

Soon I wasn't really sure any longer if I were being sustained by faith, by the grace of God, or by the sedatives! It was simple to rationalize that the pills made me a happier patient and a more pleasant person for my family to deal with.

The day came when a doctor suggested I go off the pills and didn't write the necessary prescription. That's when I learned how nerve-shattering my tremors and shakings really were! I began to sweat profusely at night, at the same time freezing under several blankets. I had dreams and nightmares although I had always insisted, "I never dream." Strange thoughts persisted in my waking hours.

I was so appalled at the ease with which I had slipped into drug dependency that I dared not go back to taking even one pill a day. Clinging to the fact that I "can do all things through the one [Christ] who keeps on pouring his power into me (Phil. 4:13)," I was able to endure the agonies of my first drug-free week. Soon I was excited that my mind was so much clearer than it had been at any time since my post-accident surgery. My mind had not been affected by the accident as I feared! This became another vibrant reason to praise God.

Mood-altering drugs, including alcohol, are among the many destructive alternatives to suicide in the face of impenetrable despair.

Escape into magic and the occult has become the contemporary "way out" for many who have lost hope. The world of illusion and unreal spirits is a never-never land where there are no real solutions. Under God's judgment (see Deut. 18), they bring only increasing depression and despair.

The most common "Christian" escape from reality is the retreat into self-pity. We have been told that it is not Christian to give in to despair; Christians are not to be depressed; they are not to be abusers of themselves with alcohol or other drugs. But Christians are also human beings with feelings, and these feelings must be expressed. Self-pity is too often the emotional expression of the pseudo-christian philosophy, *Deus vult!* (God wills it!). We resign ourselves to the will of God, but there is no joy in resignation. A sighing self-pity increases the depression of both the sufferers and those involved in their sufferings.

I found myself making statements like this to my wife.

"How can you love me now that I'm no longer the person I used to be? If you want to leave me, feel free to go. I'll understand." Naturally she protested and reassured me of her love.

To my children, I'd say, "I'm sorry you have such a dud for a father. You must get tired of waiting on me. You're young and want to have fun, and I just tie you down." Naturally they protested and reassured me of their love.

I was "bugged" by little things. When the heavy feeling on my chest and shoulders bothered me, especially in the morning, I disliked conversing and gave short, snappy answers to questions and comments from the rest of the family. I became critical of remarks which seemed inconsequential against the magnitude of my own problems. Issues that were important to them seemed trivial

24

to me, and I avoided involvement by silence or disapproval.

On the other hand, I was hurt and upset when they went on talking and left me alone. I knew they cared, but I projected my hurt onto them by saying things I knew would hurt them. Although I knew Marge was physically exhausted from caring for me, packing household goods in preparation for moving, answering correspondence, entertaining visitors, keeping the family in some semblance of a regular routine, I resented any slight inability of hers to meet my excessive demands. I felt secretly triumphant that her impatience proved I was right: I really was a burden to her, in spite of her protests!

I became frighteningly aware of my desire to remold the world around me to fulfill my new needs. To some extent we are all manipulators of those about us. That's why Paul cuts deep into our hearts when he describes pure love in 1 Cor. 13: "Love is always patient and kind. Love is never ill-mannered or irritable. Love never gives up."

I even managed to achieve some success in my attempts to manipulate others, to mold them to my plan. How easy it is to use people for your own ends when you have an emotional lever under them! We rationalize that our own ends are best and feel that our irritability is justified when others don't see things our way. We can so easily become "con" artists, conniving and scheming to make the world our kingdom, using guilt and sympathy to dominate our loved ones.

The shattering fact is that such manipulation of persons enslaves everyone, including the manipulator, and stifles the freedom essential to any joyful relationship.

For the desperate sufferer wallowing in self-pity at the foot of the mountain, hope lies in becoming motivated enough to *reach out and claim the mountain as one's own!* Contrary to resignation, which is a rejection of the mountain, the active claiming of one's situation enables one to *rejoice in the mountain.* The journey from rejection to rejoicing is found in responding to the repeated invitation of the Scriptures to "come:" "Come unto me all you who are weary and burdened." "The Spirit and the Bride say come." "Come, follow me." "Enter into the joy of your Lord."

The one in Christ must turn again to the source of strength and joy.

Is it possible to move from mere resignation to active claiming of your suffering and to find joy? Is it possible to claim your mountain with positive affirmation, "This is my own situation. God is in charge. Nothing can happen to me without his knowledge. This which seems evil must have value and worth. I am excited about its possibilities!"?

Or does that turn you off as being unrealistic?

Let me tell you how this became real for me. Marge and I were a teaching-sharing team at a retreat for 96 persons near Flint, Michigan, about a year after my accident. The schedule was heavy and taxing to my strength. I needed every ounce of my energies to be as alive as I could in presenting the riches of God's Word to that group.

During a brief break in the schedule I was studying

in the cabin assigned to us. I felt overwhelmingly inhibited by the heaviness of my body and the stiffness of my hands.

I blurted out in frustration, "God, since you've been able to heal me this far, why can't you finish the job and heal me all the way?"

In the words of the apostle who must have cried out in the same way came my answer, "I want you to remember that my grace is enough for you" (2 Cor. 12:7-9).

I knew what he meant. We are slow to believe and quick to forget. I realized that without some reminder in my body, I would soon forget that he had marvelously demonstrated his presence to me when the ocean wave broke my neck. My residual paralysis and pain would be my "thorn in the flesh" for the rest of my life to insure against my forgetting!

The whole business begins with one's acceptance of a possibility. At the bottom of the mountain receptivity opens immense possibilities. Faith releases power into the human spirit. We know we have value. We are significant in God's eyes, the One who created us male and female, in his image. He positions us center stage. Even despair and disappointment cannot thwart God.

Claiming the mountain as one's own special gift of grace transforms weakness into a door marked, ENTER GOD. From the bottom of the mountain, where the cries echo hollowly inside my loneliness, I answer, "I am here. I'm available. Lead me to your mountain."

Breaking through paralysis, pain, all physical and spiritual handicaps that strive to kill hope, we hear the voice of Jesus crying, "Rise up and walk." These words of the Savior become inside me a power-possibility. My very weaknesses become the creative sources from which my real life begins to flow. I begin to move because God invites me. My very effort brings gratification. I know that I can be a totally effective human being even if my mountain is still there every morning. Like Bonnie I start to scramble up the hill no matter what!

The mountain no longer threatens me. It's mine—and God's.

The
Climbers

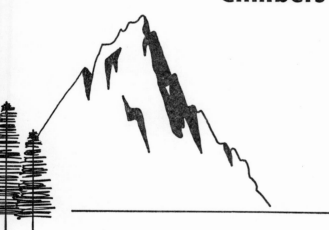

MARGE:

Erling's mountain became my mountain. I have come to realize that those who stand and walk beside those who suffer inherit their agonies.

Is the suffering of parents who watch a child die any less real than the child's pain?

Is the despair of the husband who patiently nurses a hopelessly handicapped wife any less than hers?

Are the tears that are hidden under a mask of deliberately bright cheerfulness any less bitter than those that flow openly from the loved one who needs cheering?

Is loneliness less acute for the wife who must leave her depressed husband in order to carry on the tasks of family support?

To be a true lover in Christ means to "bear one another's burdens" (Gal. 6:2). So we share the mountain, and we climb its slopes together.

And we meet many other climbers on our mountain.

I have come to think of all of us as either *uppers* or *downers*. Like mood-altering drugs we affect the spirit of the one with whom we make contact whenever we touch another life. Uppers make one feel high, downers produce a low. The warm greeting and meaningful eye contact of an upper as we pass one another on the way quickens our step and lightens our load.

(The analogy to drugs cannot be carried too far. Only the name is the same, not the total effect, since eventually both kinds of drugs are harmful.)

As Erling and I sat one day thinking about those who have, and are, climbing the mountain with us, the telephone rang. The voice on the other end of the wire faltered with weakness.

"Hi," it said, "this is Herb. I remembered that this was the week we were going to try to get together, and here I am in the hospital. I knew it would be harder for you to reach me than for me to reach you, so that's why I'm calling."

He reported that he had had surgery earlier in the week; he was doing fine; he was going home in another week and was sorry he couldn't keep his appointment with us.

After we had hung up the phone, we hugged one another and laughed out loud. We had been sitting there in that small apartment bedroom, pondering the course of our lives, fighting feelings of rejection and loneliness when Herb's call came, and the grace of shared love renewed us.

Once again, a fellow climber became an upper to us.

No one of us is always a downer or always an upper.

Some of each ingredient brews in all of us. Like yeast and salt, or grime and soot, we leave some of what we are on every person we brush against.

We are sharply aware of what it's like to be a downer. On days when we know this to be an apt description of our mood, we are likely to say, "I should never have gotten out of bed this morning."

Grumpy and out-of-sorts, we bring gloom along with us. Like a character out of the Peanuts comic-strip, we walk about with a dark cloud hanging over our heads. Woe to anyone who crosses our path on days like this!

What makes the difference in the way people affect us? Why do we get a big boost upwards from some who walk into our lives, while others send us down into the abyss?

Part of the problem lies in the fact that we don't know how to relate to people who have obvious "mountains" in their lives. How do you climb alongside of the person with terminal cancer? What kind of boost can you give to the lonely mourner whose beloved will never walk this earth again? What do you say to the one who lies helpless with paralysis?

A letter came from a friend with a request that I visit someone in the hospital. The patient, said the letter, "was stopped at an intersection and was hit from the rear by a vehicle going 65 miles per hour. She broke her neck and is completely paralyzed. This was in June. She was six months pregnant and lost her baby. She has a tracheotomy and has been on a Bennett respirator. She communicates through tongue clicks in Morse code as the hole in her throat impedes people from understanding her speech."

"Dear God," I cried, when I read that letter, "how does one walk the mountain with someone in this situation? I who can walk and talk and touch my friends—what can I possibly bring to her?"

Whatever I am is all that I have to give.

The most important characteristic of uppers is this: *they are authentically real.*

Faking good cheer and optimism is not consistent behavior for an upper. We have learned, however, to understand that the person who puts on a "front" does so out of fear of doing or saying something "wrong." The honest reaction of the real self to the shock of another's physical disability might not be very "nice" or "acceptable," one reasons. Therefore, we pretend the situation isn't as bad as it really is. We smile to cover our distress, laugh to keep from crying, and tell jokes to stay away from intimate conversation.

I remember the young pastor who came to see Erling shortly after his accident, when he was still in the Intensive Care Unit. Hospital rules permitted only one visitor at a time in the ICU. The young man was in the unit only about thirty seconds when he came out, white and obviously shaken.

"I couldn't take it," he said, "the smell, the tongs in his head—I was afraid I'd faint, or cry, or throw up, and pastors aren't supposed to act like that when they make hospital calls!"

Pastors aren't the only ones who suffer because they feel that they must act in a certain manner to be correct; most of us are trained to behave in ways that are considered acceptable to our social group. According to this code, it is more acceptable to pretend nothing is wrong and hide our real feelings. Even Christians pretend.

In fact, it may be that religious people pretend more than others. After all, isn't the Christian supposed to be able to rise above despair and nervousness and tears? If we don't manifest positive assurance in our behavior, won't people think our faith doesn't amount to much?

The tragedy of being a pretender lies in the fact that the pretense forces the other person to go along with the pretense in order to save the pretender from thinking this his phoniness is obvious. That takes so much extra energy! When words must be analyzed before they are spoken and actions must be guarded, that's work. So the pretender drains the sufferer's energies and gives nothing in return but hollow phrases and platitudes.

The implication here is not that commiseration is more desirable, but that we must somehow enter into the suffering in an authentic way in order to help get under the burden and so lighten the load.

We are able to deal with the one who comes in honesty, even if the only words that can honestly be said are these, "I really didn't want to come. I was afraid of what I would find in you. I thought you might be terribly changed or depressed and that my visit would only make things worse. I don't even know what to say but I'm here because I care about you."

If you feel like weeping, what's wrong with weeping together when the going is tough? Only don't weep "as those who have no hope," rather weep because shared tears can lift one as much as shared laughter. If tears are that day's portion of the climb, then laughing or affecting gaiety would not be authentic.

If caring and loving fill you with the need to touch and hold the climber, then yield to the impulse. The comfort of a touch or a heartfelt embrace linger long after the giver has gone. Only let the embrace be genuine! The shrinking kiss, the quick formal hug, the perfunctory touch may only serve to reinforce the sufferer's sense of loneliness and diminished self-worth.

In addition to being really *real,* one who is an upper is *sensitive to the climber's need.* The going may be so rocky on the day you choose to join in the climb that all energy is needed just for the struggle. Talking is too much; listening is impossible. Just being present then may be the biggest upper of all. To care enough to walk alongside of another, to share the same path for a piece of time—isn't this the best boost we can give each other?

Real sensitivity walked into our life in the hospital when a friend brought a unique six-inch cross which he had made from barbed wire. The symbolism of that cruel material reworked into the redemptive shape of God's love has never ceased to warm us no matter how desolate the climb. I hung it beside Erling's bed in the hospital, and now he wears it whenever he preaches. It represents so well the price Christ paid for his good news that suffering is not without meaning. That barbed wire cross has become the symbol of our climb, and a constant source of strength.

Before his accident Erling had accepted a series of

assignments at a military base in the south. When he realized that he was going to have some continuing handicap, he wanted to write to the chaplain in charge and ask to be excused from his obligation.

"Don't just say you can't come," I pleaded. "Tell him why. He may still want you. After all, can't men who know they may have to die or be maimed in the performance of their job identify more readily with someone who speaks from that perspective?"

Erling's feelings, born out of his own struggle with despair, was that he was worthless to serve the chaplain's objectives. Nevertheless, to please me, he called and explained his situation to the chaplain.

"I cannot yet button my shirt, tie my shoelaces, or do a number of other things for myself. I walk stumblingly. I'll understand if you think it best to withdraw the invitation for me to speak."

The reply came immediately.

"Just come," the chaplain said, *"I'll be your hands."*

I had dreaded his going, because it would be the first time since the accident that he would be away from home alone. I fretted, wondering how he would get along without one of us to help him. When he reported the chaplain's reply, I ceased worrying. That sensitive man was exactly the kind of upper Erling needed at that point in his climb!

But all of these are transients—they are people who come and go, touching our lives briefly with grace. It remains for us—Erling and Marge, husband and wife—to keep on learning how to walk together comfortably along this strange new path.

Our marriage contract said, "for better, for worse. . . in sickness and in health." How easily those phrases had rolled from our tongues on that long ago wedding day in a peaceful Texas hamlet called Cranfills Gap!

Today those words no longer exist just as faded print in the scrapbook of our past, but are neon-lighted in the realities of the present. "For better, for worse . . . in sickness and in health." The mountain tests our commitment to this pledge every day. There are times when we fail.

Erling's neck was broken in August, and on January 1st I began my new job in Minneapolis. For nine months we lived together in an apartment there, taking some of our household goods with us but leaving most of it in storage and the rest of it with two of our children who were going to college and sharing an apartment in California.

Every day I went to work, and at least once a week and frequently on weekends my assignments took me out of town overnight. Erling, always active and energetic, was now unable to work. His daily routine included two hours of dressing and shaving, an hour of exercising in the apartment gym, a three-block walk to the grocery store and back, washing dishes, vacuuming when necessary, reading and resting. That was it. What a change from the busy schedule of a parish pastor!

This necessary reversal of our usual roles placed great stress on our relationship. The adjustment might not have been as difficult for many other couples, especially where the wife had been accustomed to working at a job outside the home, but I had not worked for a salary since our marriage. My life had revolved around family, church, and community.

My new job was very demanding, and I would come home at dinner time totally drained of energy. At the door to our apartment I would pause and breathe a prayer for a lifting of my spirit so that I could cope with whatever emotional needs Erling had for that day.

Usually the necessary energy came as a direct realization of the pledge that the Lord would renew the strength of those who wait upon him (Isaiah 40:31b):

> They shall run and not be weary,
> they shall walk and not faint.

But even so, there were times when the pressures of my day combined with Erling's obvious despair to make me feel that he was just giving in to self-pity, and I resented that. My visible impatience only added to his depression.

I defended myself by reasoning, "After all, I don't have life easy either. Maybe his broken neck has made life tough for him, but it hasn't exactly made mine a bed of roses!"

Whenever thoughts like this came, I was immediately overcome with remorse. The last thing a person suffering any physical or emotional difficulty needs is a spouse who is a downer! Nevertheless, I developed a great deal of sympathy for the mates of the chronically ill during that year of Erling's convalescence. The moods of invalids are as unpredictable as their physical condition.

Erling admitted that at times he could not help resenting my physical health and vigor, contrasted with the clumsiness of his body. He was envious of my mobility;

I could drive a car and he couldn't. My freedom accentuated the feelings of uselessness which resulted from his virtual imprisonment in the apartment. Unable to verbalize these feelings, he withdrew into long periods of silence.

Out of our struggle to adapt to the changed circumstances of our life came new understandings of each other's previous roles. I began to empathize with all those women and men who, every day of their lives, no matter what the weather or their morning mood, must go to work in the morning and be away from home until late in the day. I understood their exhaustion at the end of each day and the feeling of being trapped by agendas that separate us from those we love.

Erling came to appreciate the fact that the life of a house-spouse does not offer unlimited rewards either. Out of his own frustration, restlessness, and boredom, he articulated these new insights.

"I'm beginning to see," he said, "why alcoholism and addiction to tranquilizers and barbituates is on the rise among middle-aged housewives, especially if they don't drive a car and if they live in apartments where every day everyone else goes off to a job somewhere else!"

The strain on our relationship was so intense at times that, except for the love we share and the forgiveness the Spirit enables us to mutually give and receive, we could never have successfully kept that blithe pledge we had made so long ago before God's marriage altar.

In addition to our commitment to our marriage, it helps that both of us are committed to the biblical principle of mutual subjection to each other's good. Paul says it so well in Ephesians 5:21: "Be subject to one another out of reverence for Christ." To us the marriage relationship does not assume the form of a ladder with higher and lower rungs of responsibility, but rather shapes itself into an equilateral triangle, with Christ himself at the very top point and wife and husband below sharing equally in the tasks of making the marriage all that it can be in Christ.

Why is this important? Because this frees us from the need to prove our sexual identities by living our sex-role stereotypes. It doesn't matter to us who earns the living in our marriage or who does the dishes. These are shared responsibilities, parts of the whole package of responsibility we both agreed to when we exchanged marriage vows.

Since life doesn't move in a neat straight line but rounds many unexpected corners, it's important that girls as well as boys learn professions and skills that will enable them to support a family if necessary, and that boys as well as girls learn to care for children and do all the other tasks necessary for the nurture of a family. This kind of role flexibility frees the marriage partners to shape a family lifestyle which is best suited to their individual temperaments and circumstances and to what they consider best for their own family.

In the long, long walk up our mountain, we really have to depend on each other every day. If *we* can't walk hand in hand, lifting each other when necessary, then the whole thing is a bad trip!

We have learned this much: we are downers to each other whenever we concentrate on our own "miseries," and we lift each other whenever we can look beyond ourselves to the other's needs. That's when we enter into the mind of Christ (Phil. 2:3-7) and that's where being an upper begins.

Above all, there is God: the God who was born into our image, who was tempted as we are tempted, who suffered as we suffer, who died as we die. That God climbs every step with us—the fellow-sufferer whose nail-pierced hands hold ours, the untiring companion of all the unknown paths that criss-cross our mountain.

The
Abyss

Erling:

The path we walk is a narrow ledge over an abyss whose dark recesses often crawl with slimy fears. The abyss is alive. It clutches suffocatingly at one's whole psyche. In it lies physical and mental torture, with all the primitive fears rising from its depths. Whatever we dread takes shadowy shape within our private abyss. Sounds, sensations, panic—all reach up to tear the climber from the ledge.

A memory from my childhood gives physical dimensions to this kind of experience. One of my boyish excitements was climbing the narrow stairs winding around the inside of the grain elevator which my father operated in our North Dakota town. Just under the roof of the soaring structure, I would edge along the catwalks which bridged the huge grain bins that rose hundreds of feet from the ground below. In the late afternoon the small apertures under the roof permitted a minimal amount of slanting light to illumine just the top of the cavernous depths below. The excitement of walking on the narrow planks was enhanced by not knowing if there was any grain at all in the bin.

I pondered, how far would I fall if I fell? What if there were no grain and the fall took me all the way to the floor below? What if the surface of the grain were far enough down so that my plunge into it would bring suffocation? What if no one heard my screams? What if . . .?

"Jump!" invited the darkness below me.

Sweat would dampen the palms of my hands and panic grip my stomach as I resisted the hypnotic tug of the pit below and inched my way to safety on the other side.

In the same way the walk on the mountain takes me daily to the edge of an abyss.

The abyss is the moment of temptation when all the powers of the Evil One are focused against us.

At the oddest times and often in the least expected moments, the hour of temptation comes. Such a moment came for me most unexpectedly eight months after the accident which broke my neck. We were guests at a benefit performance of an ice show. Walking through one of the lower level corridors of a huge sports arena, we anticipated the fun of one of our first nights out after months of confinement. Some caretaker at the arena had pulled up a steel partition which could close off the two portions of the corridor. It had not been raised far enough to permit a tall person to pass without stooping. Looking down instead of up, I did not see it in time.

Marge, suddenly aware of the danger, called, "Erling, watch out!"

But the call came too late. I raised my head just as I passed under the partition, and the sharp steel of its bottom edge cut into my scalp, jarring my head back sharply. I would have fallen if Marge and our son Erling had not caught me.

Panic and fear gripped me. "Oh God," I cried, "I've broken my neck again!"

I felt the same pain in my head and neck that permeated my whole body at the time of my first accident. I felt compressed by the fear that I had broken my neck again. A small crowd had gathered around me, and I recalled all the sensations of my previous encounter with death. This time, however, there was no experience of joy and ecstasy, only the despair of thinking that I would have to go through another agonizing hospitalization with surgery, pain, disability. I leaned against the stone block wall of the corridor, half sobbing and moaning slightly because of the pain from the cut on my head. Someone ran to report my accident to an attendant.

Marge asked if I wanted to go home, her face betraying her fears for me. Not wanting to disappoint my son, who had been looking forward to that evening, I told her that I thought I was all right and would try to stay for a while. With her support I managed to walk, and we stayed for the performance.

For me those two-and-a-half hours sitting on the edge of the glistening sheet of ice on whose surface skaters twirled and floated lightly were a journey through the abyss. I shook constantly, chilled not only by the cold which came from the ice, but mostly from the icy fingers of fear. How would this new injury affect my still precarious physical condition? Would it affect my recovery? Would paralysis return again?

In that moment I was tempted to deny both the goodness and the power of God. I felt utterly abandoned. Could he really care? Did it make any difference if he did? My first skirmish with death may have been necessary to re-awaken me to spiritual newness, but why this senseless accident?

This became my hour of temptation when the abyss yawned invitingly. God had deserted me, it seemed, and I was alone with my fears. In that moment, Satan robbed me of all my joy, all of my previous experience of the goodness of God. I was tempted to believe that everything I had known of his love was a myth, a figment of my desire to believe, a self-induced wish fulfillment. I doubted that the Word had ever been more than a pious dream in my life, a mirage in the desert of living.

I was convinced that I would never survive a collapse into what I had been before my recovery. My spirit could never cope with another battle against paralysis.

This sense of being alone in the struggle is the essence of temptation. This is the fearful abyss which leads to the denial of God. Life becomes a lonely walk through the darkness where no light is visible. The only sound is the echo of one's own cry. Like Jesus, one cries, "My God, my God, why have you forsaken me?"

Into the loneliness of that hell, Satan comes with his sly insinuation, "Has God really said . . .? Do you think God really meant it when he said he loved you? Did you really see Jesus back there in the ocean? Was your recovery from paralysis really due to prayer or to a lucky series of coincidences? If God is really watching over you, how come you're the one who always gets hurt?"

In the arena, the skaters cavorted on the ice. I dimly remember the changing sets and costumes. Clowns and comics and acrobats swirled to the beat of rhythmic music. Colored spotlights dazzled. Creeping cold came with clutching fingers. I felt encased by it. Applause beat against my eardrums, but I felt totally alone in the happy crowd, the only one I thought, who was fighting a life-and-death struggle with the Evil One.

"Trapped! Caught in the corner!" So Luther describes those who have this same feeling of desperateness, when life drops like a snare. There I sensed the supreme cunning of Satan. He has so many things going in his favor.

On the one hand, we like to be the center of attention. Temptation excites us as the old drive to "be God" surfaces. We relish the spotlight. The child in us cries out, "Look at me!"

On the other hand even the smallest weakness becomes a wedge through which the Evil One may enter. He reads me clearly. The flick of an eye, the hidden desires of my spirit, the slightest sign of weakness invites him to move in to deliver a killer blow.

Satan works on emotions to find any mood to exploit. He digs into my self-pity as my heart still cries, "Why did this happen to me?" Memories of failure vividly re-created became an open invitation to Satan's desire to make the failure become a reality again. A woman watching a television movie was overwhelmed by a revived guilt as the story unfolded an exact replay of a sin from her past.

A poor self-image that negates the image of God makes one a ready prey to temptation. Satan moves in to deceive, "Serve *me* and the kingdoms of the earth will be yours!"

Finally, as in an Edgar Allan Poe horror story, the abyss opens beneath me. My weaknesses overwhelm me, and I am drawn irresistibly by the suction of despair. *I cannot seem to extricate myself from the pit.*

As the cold wind from the ice chilled my legs, I remembered again the old woman who returned to the exercise room for the first time after a six week's absence. Now her arm was in a cast. Her face mirrored a visible unhappiness. I asked her what had happened.

She told me that she had broken her arm in a fall, but even more fearsome than that was the fact that her immobilized arm had developed the stabbing pain of arthritis. Instantly I felt sucked into the abyss of dread.

Time and time again at the edge of that abyss, I have concluded that it is totally impossible to resist, *in one's own strength,* the temptation to give in to despair, to deny the goodness of God, and to jump into the darkness below forever.

We cannot save ourselves!

As long as life moves along easily, we feel good about ourselves, about God and about the world around us. How easily the words roll from our lips, "I was tempted but didn't give in." As long as we can say that, we have not been tempted.

Temptation is only temptation when I stand at the

edge of the abyss, unable to do anything but cry out for help!

I am faced with only two options: to give up God by denying his love or to give in to God by embracing his love.

As long as I delude myself by thinking I can overcome sin and temptation in my own strength, I am always in danger from the abyss. Satan knows that *my* strength is no match for *his* powers.

The compulsive eater and drinker know this. Drug addicts fight in vain to free themselves from their bondage. Even the Christian struggles futilely against old thought patterns that are now rejected but which still return to tempt. The same old anger, impatience, greed, and covetousness destroy us day by day. Paul said, "For I do not do the good I want, but the evil I do not want is what I do" (Rom. 7:19).

Time runs out. Tiredness of living pressures us to give in. Where shall I run? Where hide from life? Where go to get away from the temptation to despair? How to keep from denying God? The depths below exert a final tug. I feel totally helpless. All I want to do is to die and be done with it.

I remembered my grain elevator experiences again. In the corner of the ground floor of that same elevator stood a separator, a rectangular automatic grain sifter. Into its mouth many times a day went a sample, properly measured and weighed, of each truck load of wheat brought in from nearby farms. When the contents had been emptied into a lower compartment, a button was pushed to begin the separation process. Violently the material was tossed up tiers of small sieves, all of which were in constant motion. No bit of the substance had a moment's rest until it reached its final destination.

In that turbulent sifting process every shriveled, dried up, incomplete kernel of grain plus all of the chaff, straw, weed seeds, and bits of sand fell through one of the sieves. These worthless particles all fell into a common drawer. They really had no value. Sometimes they were burned; sometimes they were dumpd on the ground to be food for the birds. They were always "good for nothing" in the eyes of my father, who made a business of buying wheat.

Only the mature, the intact, the whole kernel was able to fight its way to the top of the machine into the holding container for perfect grain. The eyes of everyone involved were focused only on the finished product. Seedtime and harvest had only one concern, a perfect product.

Only the whole grain of wheat will find its way to the top.

Jesus told Peter about the sifting process shortly before his crucifixion. The sense of urgency and of love for the tempestuous disciple surfaces in his double call, "Simon, Simon, *look*, Satan has *demanded* to have you, that he might sift you like wheat; but I have prayed for you that your faith may not fail; and when you have turned again, strengthen your brethren."

Only one answer has ever come that has any permanent validity. In the abyss the only hope is the Cross. And the interceding Christ.

When I hold the Cross up, show it to the tempter and claim it as my only strength and power in the night of despair, victory is mine. In my weakness, Jesus becomes strong for me. When I give in, admitting that I have no strength of my own to survive the tug of the abyss, then I am ready for grace to move in.

When I looked up in the elevator, I saw light straining to penetrate the dirtied window panes above. I recognized another world. Jesus said, "I am the light of the world" (John 9:5). The psalmist exults, "In thy light do we see light" (Ps. 36:9). Small wonder that Paul reminds us to "move out of darkness into his marvelous light!" and that Peter invites us to a "living hope," and that the saints have confessed, "Hail, O Cross, our only hope!"

The light broke in for me again in that strange experience of walking into the overhanging door. Once more I was reminded that the Cross is my strength and my hope, and it is "the power of God."

Because of it Jesus knows what every tempted one goes through; in the Garden of Gethsemane he too was tempted to give up. Because of the Cross Jesus has dedicated himself to a vocation of intercessory prayer for every one who calls upon him in the moment of temptation and despair.

The writer of Hebrews makes a strong case for the intercessory ministry of Jesus.

"For because he himself has suffered and been tempted, he is able to help those who are tempted" (2:18).

"For we have not a high priest who is unable to sympathize with our weaknesses, but one who in every respect has been tempted as we are, yet without sin. Let us then with confidence draw near to the throne of grace, that we may receive mercy and find grace to help in time of need" (4:15-16).

"Consequently he is able for all time to save those who draw near to God through him, since he always lives to make intercession for them" (7:25).

So hang in there, companions at the edge of the abyss! He knows what you're going through because he's been there himself! You say you have no strength? Claim his. You can't hold on any longer? Let go, and you'll find that he's holding you.

Jesus' cross is the only thing stronger that the power of Satan in your life. Jesus promised Peter that his faith would not fail because he, Jesus, would be praying for him in the moment of Satan's sifting. He's doing the same for you.

The moment of temptation is gone; you're on the pathway again and the abyss has been passed.

The marching song? "In the cross of Christ I glory."

The
Ascent

MARGE:

"Keep on keeping on," the wise black matron at the university told our daughter when Kristi confided to her that she was tired and ready to quit college.

"Keep on keeping on."

That's what the ascent, that daily climb up the mountain, is all about. You *endure*. Like Jesus. That was his style.

So we endure, "looking to Jesus the pioneer and perfecter of our faith, who for the joy that was set before him endured the cross" (Heb. 12:2). The one who endures; that one will receive the crown of life, says James the brother of our Lord (James 1:12), and three times the Word tolls the reminder that it's the one "who endures to the end" that will be saved (Matt. 10:22, 24:13; Mark 13:13).

It's not where or how one *starts* that matters; it's whether one makes it to the finish line. Implicit in the baptism of Jesus was the agony of the crucifixion, and every Christian baptism commits the one baptized to a participation in the death and burial of Jesus in order to also rise with him (Col. 2:12).

That fact forms the context for his question to James and John when they asked for the privilege of sitting beside him in his "glory." "Are you able to be baptized with the baptism with which I am baptized?" he probed (Mark 10:38).

According to the Scriptures the road to resurrection and glory is inevitably a cross-road, and the casualties of that rough way are those humans who just could not, for one reason or another, keep on keeping on.

But who can meet the ultimate demands of endurance, the demands

—to sustain or undergo without breaking or yielding,

—to remain firm under adversity,

—to submit with patience,

—to suffer without giving up,

—to remain in existence,

—to put up with,

—to bear,

—to last?

We who are committed to the daily ascent of the mountain of our suffering become peculiarly alert to the daily barriers placed along the way of endurance.

Like St. Theresa, the mystic, we cry, "O Lord, no wonder you have so few friends, when you treat them so hard!"

One brutal experience follows another until life becomes a dreadful anticipation. The ascent casts us in the role of Sisyphus who, according to Greek mythology, was condemned by the gods to push uphill forever a huge rock which always rolled down again.

Giving up becomes a viable option with every step.

Time magazine carried the story of Air Force Captain Edward Brudno in its June, 1973 issue. Stepping off the plane onto U.S. soil after eight years in a North Vietnam prison, he exulted, "Words like *unbelievable, exciting,* and *unreal* perfectly describe the fantastic excitement of being reborn!"

Only a month later he added, "I knew the initial euphoria would pass, and it has."

Then he told a friend, "I'm feeling pretty depressed these days."

His despair deepened. His wife had become anti-war. He wondered what he had fought for and saw no reason for going on. Under this stress, the fear and despair that he had lived with in the years of captivity once again reclaimed him. Soon he was taking sleeping pills; one day he took too many.

By a miracle of God's grace those first months after Erling broke his neck were sheer ecstasy. The love and prayers of many people supported us. It was only natural that, as the gravity of his condition lessened, the full force of all that multiplied prayer concern shifted to others experiencing more immediate needs. The focus of love must necessarily shift to those whose needs are the most intense: those who *today* are under unbearable stress, those who *today* have obvious needs.

Today's prayers must be matched to today's needs.

Unfortunately for the climber, however, the ascent

often appears most steep when one's needs become less apparent to the observer. For us that time came when Erling returned to California while I remained in Minneapolis.

Why did he leave? Because he recovered from his paralysis. By September a year later, he was wonderfully, miraculously well enough to go back to work! St. Olaf, the church he was serving when he was hurt, had given him a year's leave of absence. For them it was a gesture of great love. None of us knew if he would ever be able to return to his ministry again when we left for Minneapolis.

But one year after his crippling, he felt ready to go back. Although he was still fighting for movement every morning, he was able to work a full day without having to stop and rest; the neck brace was never necessary; his steps were steadier; and his voice had just about returned to its former full quality and volume. Our fifteen-year-old son decided that he wanted to return to California with his father in order to join his high-school classmates.

I had never lived alone, and I had never wanted to live alone, so when I stood watching the plane which was taking my husband and my youngest child to a home two thousand miles away from me, despair overwhelmed me. No other circumstance during that year had made me feel so desolate.

I was reminded of those news stories telling about the reactions of London children to the bombings of that city during World War II. Those who remained in London with their parents survived the horrors of the bombings with much less emotional damage than those who were sent to the country for safekeeping with kindly strangers. Separation anxiety caused them more suffering than if they had remained at home and shared the bombing raids with their families.

Erling and I had drawn strength from each other through all of our trials and felt that together we could handle whatever came, but separation was something we had never known except for brief periods of time. Now the prospect of being apart indefinitely frightened both of us, and doubts came.

After thirty-one years of marriage, how could we stand to have separation added to all the other distresses of that year?

What purpose could being apart possibly serve?

Out of our year of separation, certain learnings have come. The first of these convictions is that nothing and no one can ever take the place of the person with whom one has become "one flesh" in a marriage that has been put together by God. Dietrich Bonhoeffer articulated this fact so well when he wrote from his cell in a Nazi prison during World War II about being separated from loved ones:

> In the first place nothing can fill the gap when we are away from those we love, and it would be wrong to try and find anything. We must simply hold out and win through. It is nonsense to say that God fills that gap; he does not fill it, but keeps it empty so that our communion with another may be kept alive, even at the cost of

pain. . . . We must not wallow in our memories or surrender to them, just as we don't gaze at a valuable present, but get it out from time to time, and for the rest hide it away as treasure we know is there all the time.

Aloneness puts additional stress on endurance, but the requirement to endure is still there.

We have worked out some survival techniques to help us "keep on keeping on" when we're out on the sheer rock wall of the mountain—alone. We share them in the hope that others may find them helpful.

Survival technique number one: Think NOW.

Don't look up or down, backward or forward. Just concentrate on what must be done at the present moment.

We've learned that when we dwell on the past or worry about the future, we end up being ineffective in the present. When Erling's paralysis changed his physical performance for the remainder of his life, the "good old days" were gone forever for us. Never again would we run together on the beach, climb a hill, or play tennis.

The past exists only in our memories. Dwelling on what used to be destroys the present for us and for those around us. Does anyone enjoy the "bore" who is forever talking about the way things used to be? Do those persons really enjoy themselves?

If only statements still come to mind. *If only* we hadn't gone to the beach that day. *If only* Erling had stayed out of the water. *If only* I had found a job in California so we wouldn't have to be separated. *If only* his disability hadn't rendered him sensitive to cold temperatures. *If only. . . .*

I have listened to individuals blaming themselves unmercifully for their sins and decisions of the past. That seems such a waste of energy! So many are living with guilts that they should never have assumed in the first place: for not having gone to college and so displeasing their parents, for not having been there when a parent died, for not having obeyed grandma, and so on. These feelings must be dealt with for what they are—unreal ghosts from the past—and then *consciously* forgotten.

Even the real burdens we bear from our pasts need to be confessed and then left with Jesus, the Lamb of God who takes up and bears away our sins. The Word assures us that God remembers our sins no more, but puts them from him as far as the east is from the west (Ps. 103:12): that he drowns them in the depths of the sea and the place that swallows them doesn't even remember that they are there (Mic. 7:19).

Hanging on to what God has already removed becomes a way of denying responsibility for actions in the present. If I keep on beating myself emotionally for what I did on one of my yesterdays, it may keep me from having to face the reality of what I'm doing *now*.

My guilt feelings are then spent on irrevocable deeds from my past rather than being permitted to work to change my behavior in the present.

This constant reexamination of past misdeeds may be the ultimate denial of God's forgiving grace and love, because it denies that the Cross has power in *all* cases. There is no sinner or sin outside of God's forgiveness!

Haven't you heard people say, "Well, I'm so bad that nothing I do now can make things any worse, so there's no use even trying!"

It's one way of refusing to take seriously the words of Jesus when he says, "Your sins are forgiven. Go your way and sin no more" (John 5:14; 8:11).

So looking back down the mountain does not help us come to terms with the place where we are now. Like Lot's wife (Gen. 19) we could remain fixed forever with a backward glance.

Looking anxiously to the future doesn't help us either. Mists shroud the road ahead, and even the next hour is really not ours. Just as pining for a lost past sours life in the present, so does fearing the future.

Anxiety forms with the words *what if*. *What if* I quit my job and then find out that Erling cannot go on working. *What if* our relationship changes because of our absence from one another. *What if* our children develop emotional problems because we don't have a "normal" home life. *What if* we begin to enjoy being apart. *What if* loneliness drives us to do something desperate. *What if* I crack up. *What if. . . .*

The future is not here and it may never come. To worry about it brings all of the fear and feelings of depression, but none of the strength that God has promised for each day (Deut. 33:25). And didn't Jesus say that each day's troubles belong to that day, so therefore don't be anxious about tomorrow because tomorrow will look after itself (Matt. 6:34)?

One learns on the mountain ascent to deal only with the path on which one walks at the present. Only the rock underfoot needs to be stepped over or gone around —not the one two feet ahead. Only the climate of *this* place needs to be endured or enjoyed—not the forecast for tomorrow.

Besides loneliness for my husband, the second most dominant emotion during the time of my separation was anxiety for my fifteen-year-old son. Worry about what might be happening to him in my absence almost consumed me. If I heard that he was planning a trip into the mountains late at night with an astronomy class, I fretted that he might be riding with a careless driver. If a letter came saying he had the flu, guilt about not being there to give him tender loving care nagged at me.

It took conscious effort to make myself concentrate on the tasks of my job assignment rather than wasting that energy in pointless worrying about a situation which worry could not help. Maybe that's a special problem of mothers. We tend to believe that fathers can't do as good a job of parenting as we can. I had to learn that this precious son could get along just as well with the concerned companionship of his father as with me.

To learn to live with the tasks of today and the possibilities of the present situation is a necessary technique for survival on the ascent.

Survival technique number two: Think thanks.

"What is it in your present situation for which you can thank God?" This is the first question I ask myself whenever anxiety starts to dog my footsteps on the mountain.

We were to discover that it's a good deal more difficult to find cause for thanksgiving when we're separated than when we're together. But overwhelmingly, two facts presented themselves as reasons for daily rejoicing.

First of all, we could arise every morning articulating this prayer, "I thank you, God, that the reason we are separated is because Erling got well!" After all, if he had remained paralyzed, he could not have gone back to work. Who could possibly not rejoice in a separation which had this fact as its cause?

There was a time in my life when I could not bear to see Erling leave home. Panic gripped me whenever he drove away or flew off in a plane. Left alone with my three preschoolers, I felt trapped and helpless. An unhealthy dependency enslaved me.

That was a number of years ago, but it was during that period that some of these survival techniques began to take shape for me. When one of our congregations voted to give Erling a world mission tour as a gift—a tour which took him away from us for eight weeks and left me alone with our five young children—I began to apply the "thank" principle in a serious way to my own situation. I had always affirmed Phil. 4:6-7 as a happy prayer possibility but then I decided to test it as a practical axiom for solving "problems" like mine.

I did this: whenever I thought about Erling's impending mission tour and anxiety squeezed my stomach with the familiar *what if* questions, I immediately began to pray in this way.

"Lord, I thank you that you are giving Erling this great opportunity to learn more about the people in your world, and I also thank you that you are giving me this opportunity to grow in independence."

It worked! Gradually as this prayer became habitual, the anxiety dissipated and joy and peace took its place. That summer while Erling was gone, I found myself involved in all sorts of unexpected activities, including trips with the children, new study projects, and an invitation to write a film script. In fact it worked so well that I almost felt guilty because I hadn't worried at all about his being gone or about my being alone.

When we learn to give thanks in all things, then God's peace is set free to stand guard over our "hearts" and "minds." Conscious effort is necessary until thanksgiving becomes a habit.

So, consciously, every day I find it necessary to give thanks in these words, "Lord, I thank you that the reason my husband and I are not able to be together is that he got well and was able to go back to work!"

Then I can praise God and find peace.

Survival technique number three: Think selectively

The mind can only be tuned in to one thought at a time. It selects a picture or a train of thought to focus on.

Thoughts that bring in their wake feelings of nervousness, self-pity, depression, panic, and fear need to be *consciously* tuned out. Learning that it's within one's powers to do this is a remarkably liberating discovery!

Then you are no longer the *victim* of your own mind.

But so many people have said to me words like this whenever I've suggested that they can take charge of their own thoughts, "But I can't *help* it! Whenever I start thinking about (and then they name some anxiety-producing situation in their own life), I begin to feel nervous, and one thought leads to another and before you know it, I'm so depressed that I have to run for help!"

I don't want to imply that taking charge of one's life and thoughts is a simple matter, since it really involves the entire process of growing from birth to adulthood. Nevertheless the healthy individual need not be victimized by unhealthy thought patterns.

Think of it this way. Your mind focuses on one thought at a time. The time it gives to that thought may be brief before it hastens on to the next one. For some well-meaning person to tell you to "think positive thoughts" when your mind is running around that nervous racetrack does not help one bit! Especially when you know that certain worrisome thoughts are always on a collision course with panic and fear.

Let me share my survival technique for the control of worry.

When burdens pile high and the way grows steep, worry moves in as a permanent resident in the mind— thoughts slip into the worry "groove" automatically, each time making the worry groove a little deeper. Somehow they must be prevented from pursuing their dreary unproductive course toward uncontrolled panic.

Now one of the great gifts God has given us is the ability to forget. Without that faculty our minds would cling forever to every memory, good or bad. We'd like to forget the bad and remember the good.

The problem then is to assist the forgetting process when we need to get rid of destructive worry thoughts. Remember that the mind can focus on only one thought at a time and that thought triggers a good emotional response or a bad emotional response.

This is where conscious effort is necessary. To say, "Think positive thoughts," is too general. But to think *one thought* that is a sure-fire trigger for a good emotional response is a definite possibility. So pull out of your memory file one picture from your past that always makes you feel good. For most of us it's a picture from our childhood. Even with a bad childhood environment and poor home life, children seem to find ways of having fun!

Pick out one then, and only one, such picture from your childhood. Could it be a time when you went walking through ditches full of hip-high snow on your way to school? How about that time you hunted for shells along the seashore and the sands warmed your bare feet? Remember how it felt to fly a kite on a windy day in the spring? Remember the pure joy of the first time you could roller skate or ride a two-wheeler?

Remembering, you feel better. The trick lies in keeping that *one* good picture on ready reference so you can immediately switch your mind from the worry-producing picture to the good-feeling picture, as soon as the worry one starts focusing in consciousness. Substitute it right away!

Gradually the memory of that worry-producing thought will grow dim and you'll find it easier and easier to substitute the helpful thought. You've substituted a positive thought groove for a negative one.

Are you running away from reality if you do this? No, you are simply substituting one reality for another.

Anxiety is only good when it can lead to constructive problem solving. When it becomes an end in itself, it's not only worthless, but harmful.

So think—selectively. In Philippians, Paul says it this way, "Whatever is true, . . . honorable, . . . just, . . . pure, . . . lovely, . . . gracious, if there is any excellence, if there is anything worthy of praise, think about these things" (Phil. 4:8).

Survival technique number four: Think expectantly.

God is a God of surprise.

That's the message of Christmas and Easter. Christmas says to a world longing for the appearance of the Almighty One, "Here is a baby; worship him. He's the Mighty God, the Everlasting Father, the Prince of Peace."

What surprise! Joy breaks into a weary world, angels sing and wise men bend low. Surprise!

To Mary Magdalene weeping at the tomb of the dead Savior, the Risen Lord appears. Death gives way to life! Surprise!

As I faced the loneliness of my stay in Minneapolis, God surprised me by giving me a son to live with me. That fall Steve enrolled as a student at Luther Theological Seminary in St. Paul.

Live on tiptoe, expecting God to surprise you with joy. The promise Jesus makes is that he will not leave us orphans but will send us a Comforter.

On the steep rock wall of your mountain, he comes to walk with you.

And you will endure!

The
Equipment

ERLING:

"Straight below us—1,600 feet of empty air. Above us—4000 feet of perpendicular granite." So begins the gripping story in the June, 1974, issue of *National Geographic* magazine of three intrepid adventurers who were "proud right down to the marrow of our aching bones" at scaling Yosemite's famed Half Dome. The danger of their climb was enhanced by their decision to use little aluminum wedges and nuts called "chocks" as their anchors and fall stoppers. On such anchors, some no larger than a child's thumbnail, which they popped into cracks in the sheer walls they were climbing, they "staked our climb, our hopes, and our lives," they said. In addition they used ropes, steel loops thinner than a shoelace, mountain boots, giant safety-pins. But to them, as rock climbers, the ascent's appeal proved irresistible.

My heart only echoes their confession. On the same kind of tools I, too, stake my "climb, my hopes, and my life." Little aluminum wedges in the shape of positive words support my ascent. Thin rays of encouragement in the eyes of others become steel loops in which to anchor a foothold.

A doctor gave me the first of these little wedges of support when, at a crucial point in my recovery, I was sent to a famous university hospital for an analysis of my condition.

Still confined in the restrictive brace that inhibited my breathing and my movements, my heart longed for the day that I could be released from it. The second-ranking specialist in physical medicine at the university began his check of my body. Soon he was to share three sentences that provided me not only exciting but supportive words.

First, with widely smiling face he unveiled his first conviction: "You are a phenomenon!"

I knew what he meant, but I translated his words in my own terms and out of my own personal convictions as, "God has done a remarkable thing in you!" Only the Lord can heal "all of our diseases." So I could tell him that, thank God, and take renewed courage.

Second, he said, "You tell me that there were about ten persons involved in that series of ocean accidents; two were killed, and of the other eight you think only three of you are now mobile. Without question a good part of your recovery can be laid to the fact that you *were able to face up to and to cope with your problem.*"

Third, the doctor pinpointed my basic need brusquely, concisely, convincingly: "Take your brace off! Consider yourself whole!"

Transforming, healing, revolutionary, life-changing words! All kinds of lights exploded into brilliance inside my mind.

The doctor wanted me to break forth from my cocoon —literally and figuratively—by taking hold of my most effective piece of equipment, my own inner conviction of wholeness. His words were as freeing as the gospel! Memory recalled the words of an old hymn,

> Oh, wonderful words of the Gospel,
> A message of blessing they bring;
> Proclaiming a finished redemption
> Through Jesus our Savior and King."

The good news moves in as a self-releasing power when it's appropriated. The exhilaration of that possibility intrigued me: I could get out of my straight jacket. I could shed the fears of what would happen if it came off, get out from under the depressions that had slipped in from my physical hurts, cast off the self-rejection that moved in with feelings of being sick, unwhole, defeated.

The doctor knew that I had to burst out of my confining emotional cocoon if I were ever to fly again.

I must accept my wholeness—whatever that wholeness was for me—or never get beyond the plaguing question, "Do I dare take the neck brace off?"

After many months of knowing its rigid security, did I really want to be released from it into the uneasiness of possible added injury? Did I really care to take the risk?

I discovered the relevance of Paul's statements in Ephesians; some things must be "put off" before others can be "put on." Jesus stings would-be climbers with the same tormenting question he put to the man who had lain beside a pool for thirty-eight years, "Do you want to be whole?" (John 5:6). When we've grown accustomed to being chained by apathy, weakness, self-pity or sin, we can easily cop-out, "I just can't make it. I'm doomed to failure. I'm a born loser!"

A musical friend of mine wrote a western ballad when the highway department took his land, "That old house has got to go 'cause the freeway's comin' through!" A lot of things that get in my way will just have to go, not least of all the feelings of being a "sick" person. Whatever I am, that's "wholeness" for me!

Susanna Wesley once told her son John, who would one day become the founder of the Methodist Church, "Take this rule: Whatever impairs the tenderness of your conscience, obscures your sense of God, or takes the relish off spiritual things, that is sin to you, however innocent it may seem to be in itself." God's power cannot surge through me if I nourish my weaknesses. Channels must be kept open and clean.

"If we confess our sins, he is faithful and just to forgive us our sins and cleanse us from all unrighteousness" (1 John 1:9).

Have I accepted my wholeness and forgiveness? Or do I do as a friend did with another's cremated remains? He had been asked to take the ashes of a stranger on a trans-Atlantic boat from New York to London. He carefully deposited the box filled with the ashes inside his stateroom closet. Repeatedly during the journey, however, he kept taking the box out and looking at it, thinking about what that person must have been like. But ashes, like sins, he finally decided, were meant to be buried so the living can go on with life. He dropped the ashes into the sea, and life went on for him.

Unblocking channels was a spring pastime when I was a boy in the Dakotas. Spring came as a longed-for, magnificent gift. How delightful the warm, freeing air that came cascading in to transform the cold blue bleakness of winter into the first signs of blossoming life. As snow and ice began to melt, I discovered sheer joy in walking the fields around our town and coming upon little bodies of water blocked up somewhere, seemingly longing to be released. As I happily removed the barrier that held them back, a gurgling song always arose from the waters as they began to flow again.

They were not meant to be dammed up; they were destined to flow freely. As they made their way into minor, then major, streams back to the gulf and on into the ocean, only then could they be brought back by the lifting power of the sun to begin their mysterious return again to replenish the earth as snow and rains. To experience freedom, you must remove the hindrances. That kind of release is available in Jesus, because it's for freedom that Christ has "set us free" (Gal. 5:1).

The next bit of equipment I desperately need are the gospel promises. In them I experience the spiritual energies of the age to come *now*. On the printed page words seem powerless things made of ink, but they have provided me with both the formula and the dynamism for continuing my climb. The word, "I can do all things through Christ who keeps on empowering me" (Phil.

4:19), has been my lifetime battery. So much available power surges in God's promises waiting only to be released.

How much persuasion Jesus put on the words he shares! "He that has ears, let him hear!" The prophet Jeremiah was told to eat, to chew on, God's words. God wanted his thoughts to completely invade the prophet's being. As God became flesh and lived among us, words must become flesh and start living in us.

Reading about the biblical people who scaled their mountains in the past renews my strength. The historic books of the Old Testament bring to life others who experienced the awesome moment when the "Spirit of the Lord is upon me and he has anointed me to speak." I saw them, challengers of the Way, just as devastatingly sinful, as despondently despairing, as I. They were men and women with the marks of their humanity on them, but they committed themselves to God. In spite of who they were, they believed.

They got into God's promises. The words were permitted to twirl and twine about their spirits and literally captured them. Only then did they dare risk the journey. Only then did they feel the joy that floods one when he lets divine power flex muscles and wills.

They experienced the fact that what God promises, he fulfills.

Words, if true and believed, can be a revolutionary power. The doctor's words kept pounding in my mind, "Consider yourself whole. You're healed!" I needed their support.

When I began vigorous physical workouts for the first

time after my braces were removed, I was frightened. Unused muscles rebelled. I dreaded wrenching something loose in my back. My mind begged me to restrict my activity. When I pushed hard at a daily exercise routine, I occasionally developed a side paralysis that lingered for a week.

If I hadn't trusted the physician's governing word, I would never have ventured out. But I saw the strengthening gleam in his eyes, and I believed the words that he spoke. They worked. So do the words of Jesus.

An awe still envelopes me as I write this on a Sunday afternoon. The sheer realism of the Presence of Jesus has almost overwhelmed me. Today I was permitted to talk about my Lord for almost two solid hours. The excitement got into my very bones. What a Christ, my heart sang! And what promises!

The Bible verifies itself. Intuitively, instinctively, my heart rocks with the wonder of its truth. What a lift for the journey; what "chocks" to climb on! Why don't I use it more? Yesterday I soaked up page after page of it. The halo lingers even today. Delight! Dynamite! Desire! I want to keep climbing toward the summit.

Besides the words of Jesus, caring persons become ever more central to my well-being. The three who climbed Yosemite's Half Dome depended totally on one another. Each one checked the other's qualifications before entrusting his life to him. Caring people warm one like the wood stove in a Colorado home that a couple wrote me about. The stove, standing in the middle of the living room, proved to be the only means of heating the whole house in which they lived. It was enough.

The revitalizing warmth of love and joy, tenderness and care, the ecstasy of deep companionship, and moments of radiant leisure with those I love provide the person-to-person support essential for scaling the heights.

Besides words and persons, a third fascinating reality comes alive for me each day as I become increasingly sensitive to the person of the Holy Spirit. Christ's "other ego," his presence throbs in the Bible, even as he is vibrantly alive in his world. Defined as either a whisper or a roar of wind, the Holy Spirit comes with dynamic power. St. Paul recognizes his divine might visibly let loose in creation.

Creative mysteries awe us all: our universe has at least ten-to-the-28th-power octillion stars "out there" whirling in perfect timing through space. Three hundred thousand varieties of butterflies are to be found just on our little earth. We marvel at marvels unfolding.

But these are not the focus of that New Testament writer when he unveils for us the mystery of God's ultimate omnipotence. For Paul the supreme place where it all comes together is in the resurrection of Jesus Christ from the dead (Eph. 1:19-20). For Paul, nothing can top that.

The Spirit ripping the dead one away from death is the ultimate.

This is the power-possibility the Spirit wants to make available to the people of God.

Jesus used this same resurrection power so effectively in his daily ministry. Amazement struck me when I traced how dependent he let himself be on the guidance of the Spirit. Luke reveals him as "filled with the Spirit"

80

(4:1); "led by the Spirit," (4:2); "filled with joy by the Spirit" (10:21); confessing that "the Spirit of the Lord has been given to me, for he has anointed me" (4:18); ministering "with the power of the Spirit in him" (4:14). Every moment of his ministry came out of the invisible Spirit's guidance.

Out of the context of his own experience and on the eve of his ascension, Jesus provided a double pledge: first, he promised his continuing presence with his own ("Lo, I am with you always," Matt. 28:20) and then the dynamic empowering of his Spirit ("You will receive power when the Holy Spirit comes upon you!" Acts 1:8).

Even a quick glance into the chief New Testament book on the Spirit, Acts, reveals the Spirit invading the lives of ordinary people like us and transforming them into transparencies of Christ. So charged were many that we see them bursting out upon their world with a rare boldness and raw courage that still overwhelm us.

In the grip of this spiritual power they first rub their eyes in amazement and then dare risk their lives in a fervent attempt to live to "the praise of his glory" in an unbelievable joy. Many have testified that the first Christians shocked their world by outliving it, outfighting it, and outdying it. They were alive, intoxicated, filled with the glorious life of God! I know what they knew. I have experienced moments of that same power.

Nothing else more effectively equips us for living than the Spirit. He comes with a horn of plenty loaded full of gifts, talents, and tools. More than two dozen gifts are listed in the New Testament and these are merely suggestive.

In 1 Cor. 12, Paul says the Spirit gives a variety of gifts "for the common good" (v. 7), equipment to be used in helping one another along the way. Among them are the speaking of wisdom, the speaking of knowledge, faith, healing, working of miracles, prophecy, distinguishing between spirits, various kinds of tongues, and interpretation of tongues.

In Eph. 4, certain offices are designated by the Spirit to enable some persons to have as their special function the equipping of Christians for their walk and work. These "office" gifts are apostles, prophets, evangelists, pastors, and teachers.

In Rom. 12, there is another listing which includes in addition to the above, serving, exhorting, contributing with liberality, giving zealous aid, and doing acts of mercy with cheerfulness.

Now in all of these chapters stress is placed not on the *individual* but on the *community*. Individuals receive the gifts but the community is the beneficiary.

God's spiritual symphony, his church, does its music best when all of the instruments are brought into play. "Earnestly desire" these "chocks," these climbing tools of service, these gifts, encourages St. Paul. Be sure you use them for everybody's good!

When gifts for the climb are discovered and used, the whole family blesses itself and radiates love. A Sunday school superintendent sitting beside me at a dinner pulsed with a fascinating gift of leadership. Her entire staff so obviously appreciated her as a reinforcer and guide that I was blessed by being close to her.

My own heart smites me when I know that even in the

face of my abysmal and apparent weaknesses I have looked with benign indifference on the gifts the Spirit offers. No wonder lethargy, listlessness, dullness, and powerlessness fairly submerge us! So many yearn for a new spiritual drive, but sheer joy can grip me only when I am in dead earnest to be on my way and willingly open myself to all the Spirit offers to make that possible.

Who qualifies for the gifts? Actually, anyone who *wants* them (see Cor. 12:31). So generous is our God that the day of Pentecost saw a fulfillment of Joel's prophecy that God would pour out his Spirit upon "all flesh." The Spirit knows no barriers of race, economic class, sex or age, living liberally in and through both women and men, both young and old, both poor and rich (Acts 2:17-18). Each member of the Christian community can, in the Spirit, be blessed and a blessing.

Finally, the gift that permeates all gifts and holds me to my ultimate goal: hope. When my doctor asked me a final question, it struck me as deeply comical: "What are your expectations?"

From long experience he knew that "hoping is coping." Perseverance only holds us to our course when we sense the immense lift of hope. Hope makes me capable of enduring the most incredible of human demands in order that I may endure to the end and be saved.

What do I expect?

I pondered this question long after I left the doctor's office. While I hoped for a return to all that I used to be, I could not live with false hope, either. My expectations had to be tailored to the reality of my changed body.

It was Marge who turned my expectations into other

directions and lifted my hopes. She pointed to the fact that my life to this point had been lived with abundant *physical* energy.

"You've always been so busy running at top speed physically that you've never taken time to explore all of your innerness," she suggested. "Who knows what you're capable of producing if you concentrate on developing your inner resources fully?"

When I faced the fact that my hands were permanently incapable of fine manipulation, I feared I might never even be able to preach again, and preaching seems to be an essential part of a pastor's job. I had always done my thinking and writing with my fingertips on the typewriter keys. Remembering her words I set about developing the ability to "write" my sermons in my mind and have discovered a facility in preaching without notes that I might otherwise never have known!

So I make my way up my mountain, using all of the gifts provided by my Lord. I find courage in another climber that I saw on an ascending road in Tokyo. He was the last carrier of the flame being brought from Greece all the way to the Olympics. Trapped as I was in a snarl of traffic, I caught a commanding view as he swept by, churning and fighting his way the last short distance to the heights where, igniting the flame, he would usher in the global event. His face may have been contorted with pain, his body tensed for the last drive, but ecstasy flamed in his eyes as, jaws set, he swept by me with his high-held torch.

It helps me to remember him.

The
Plateau

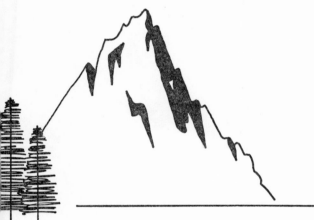

MARGE:

Even on the mountain good times come. Unexpectedly we come upon a grassy plateau where cattle graze peacefully and flowers wave in the gentle breeze. We marvel that such a place nestles among the rocky slopes.

For a kindly moment we rest. Praise flows unforced; we feel good and are convinced that we're making it.

So it was that after months of struggle and uncertainty Erling and I began to see progress in our mountain ascent. We could stop for a while, look back and say, "It's been worth it. We've come a long way. We haven't arrived, but we've made some good strides toward wholeness."

Even though Erling still fought his daily battle with resistant muscles, and we both fought to adjust to a whole new lifestyle, nevertheless a year and a half after his accident we looked out upon a level plain.

On that plateau we took inventory of our experiences, adding up our learnings along the way.

For a full year after his paralysis Erling did not drive a car.

"You drive," he'd say, "I don't feel emotionally up to it."

He feared injury if an accident should occur, and he did not trust his impaired reflexes to prevent one if he got caught in a tight spot. As long as he lived with me in Minneapolis there was no problem. I was there to do all the necessary driving.

When he moved back to California, the situation changed. Without me around and without public transportation available, he was faced with the necessity of driving a car himself or not being able to function as a pastor. Within a week after his return to the parish, he was not only driving a car, but the car was a model with a stick shift!

Even though separation had made the ascent steeper in some ways, it had forced us into new levels of growth. When Erling wrote describing the ease with which he had gone back to chauffeuring himself about, I knew that our temporary separation was a good thing. It had catapulted him to the next plateau where he could begin to feel good about himself as a whole human being.

That's how I define the plateau—as those times when we feel good about who and where we are. Like a sign pointing the way to a REST STOP the plateau invites us to rest a while from the slopes and to take time out to think about where we are in the struggle. In his return to driving a car, Erling could feel good about the long,

long way he had traveled from total paralysis. Resting and rejoicing characterize the plateau; all is *shalom.*

Shalom! Amazing word, it means salvation and wholeness and health and prosperity and peace. But above all, *wholeness.* A Hebrew word, it's pronounced as the benediction over every worshipping congregation:

> The Lord bless you and keep you;
> The Lord make his face shine upon you
>   and be gracious unto you;
> The Lord lift up his countenance upon you,
>   and give you *shalom* [peace].
>
> (Numbers 6:24-26)

Basically peace is a gift of God. Paul always links it with grace in the salutations in his epistles: "Grace and peace be unto you from God the Father and from our Lord and Savior Jesus Christ."

A gift of God, *shalom* was given as physical well-being to Erling when a specialist in physical medicine who examined him at the University of Minnesota Hospital told him a year after his injury, "You're a phenomenon! Consider yourself whole!"

What a gift! "Consider yourself whole!" God's salvation is like that. From the Latin word, *salus,* it has the double meaning of "escape from danger" and "health." In the Greek language a word with the same meanings is the word *holos,* but it also adds the concept of completeness and entirety. From it come the words *holy* and *wholly* and there you have that idea of *wholeness* again!

The plateau is *shalom.* Salvation. Peace. Wholeness.

From the time the doctor pronounced those words of wholeness over Erling, he moved steadily toward their realization. And his *shalom*-plateau came when he could drive his car again.

As for me, a person who had never liked being alone, I found myself on a plateau where I could celebrate the discovery that I enjoyed my own company! This statement may have a self-centered ring to it, but as I thought about my new feelings, I realized that people cannot really be helpful or loving to others until they learn to like their own company.

To be able to feel good when I'm alone with myself makes me better able to feel good when I'm with others. In order to experience this kind of happy wholeness I had to be thrown into a situation where I was forced to depend on myself for decision making and for taking charge of my own movements.

Aloneness frightens most of us. For me, being forced to be alone was like a wilderness wandering.

Like most middle-class women, I had moved from one sheltered environment to another. My parents were loving, concerned people who took their responsibilities seriously. Affection flowed freely from them to each one of us eight children. We never doubted their love for us and knew that we were always welcomed home. That's a good, warm, whole feeling. The Christian college I attended provided the same kind of protective environment.

Then I married Erling, a warm and compassionate person who tends to assume parental responsibility for other people. It was easy for me to let him take over most of the decision making. He did our shopping, paid the bills, took care of financial matters, and generally managed our lives. Since I enjoyed such occupations as reading, playing the piano, writing, and being with our children, I was happy to let him do it. In fact I may have pushed my share of responsibility off on to him.

Fortunately for me, however, I had been forced by Erling's growing number of assignments away from home to become somewhat knowledgeable about our business affairs and gradually accepted those responsibilities. Later, my concern for families who needed help with the care of their children motivated me to organize parish day-care centers for preschoolers. In order to administer those programs it was necessary for me to develop some management skills.

So when Erling's accident forced me to assume responsibility for the support of our family, I was somewhat prepared to assume the management job which became available to me. But like most women who for many years have not competed in that world outside the home, I had many doubts about my ability to meet the challenges. I wasn't at all sure I could make it "on my own."

Some of the doubts that bothered me were these: Could I travel alone without my husband to make all of the arrangements and to provide a sense of security in strange places and situations? Could I handle budgets, staff responsibilities, working relationships with other persons? Could I keep from being totally overwhelmed by all of those frighteningly sophisticated and intelligent people who, I had been led to believe by rumor and reading, existed out there in the world beyond the parsonage?

The process of learning that I *could* manage to make my own arrangements and to handle my own affairs became a liberating experience. A new peace, the *shalom* of wholeness, possessed me with the growing confidence that I was a whole person in my own right apart from other relationships.

I appropriated the words the doctor had said to Erling, "Consider yourself whole!" It reaffirmed Jesus' promise, "Your faith has made you whole!"

In my travels among groups of women both in and out of the church, I began to realize that most women have fears similar to mine. The "just-a-housewife" syndrome holds them captive with feelings of inadequacy and incompetency.

Assuring women that the competency needed to manage life in the home is no less than that needed outside the home has been rewarding for me. It's just a matter of motivation. Unfortunately most women are not motivated to develop the skills necessary to lead an independent existence until life forces them to be on their own.

Some never make it when that happens. Divorce or widowhood thrusts them into a frightening world of aloneness where there is no alternative but to become dependent on other more or less caring people. They become, in their own words, "burdens" to others. The loving husbands and children who "did everything" for them are seen in retrospect as not having been quite as loving as they thought themselves to be.

Many widows have confessed to me that their husbands did not want them to learn to drive the car or write their own checks. "There's no need for you to bother about things like that," they had said. "As long as I'm around, I'll take care of you."

The problem for the dependent woman comes, if not sooner, then most certainly when the husband is no longer "around." The car then sits unused in the garage, and the widow, convinced that she is not competent enough to learn to drive it, keeps it polished and tuned up in the vain hope that "some day" she'll get up enough courage to try to learn.

Because she was "protected" from business matters, someone else must assume power-of-attorney over her affairs and, willingly or unwillingly, she remains forever dependent on other people. Like children they need to be cared for by others, subject to decisions which do not reflect their own wishes. I have listened to such women as they've poured out their fears and the gnawing anxiety that grips them whenever they think about the possibility that those who support them emotionally and physically might one day abandon them.

Husbands and friends of helpless women must encourage them early in life to develop the skills which will enable them to cope with life. Love should have as its aim the highest good of the other person, and self-sufficiency is a very important "good."

God says his aim for us is that we all become "mature" in Christ (Eph. 4:13) and that we move on from simple things to "maturity" (Heb. 6:1). While we are to retain a childlike faith, we are instructed to move away from childishness in our relationships (1 Cor. 13).

Then we can relate to others out of our wholeness rather than out of our dependence and need, and that fact frees both them and us.

Sometimes it takes very little to help someone along that road to wholeness. I recall the story my friend Lia told me. Waiting at a bus stop one day, she noticed a lovely, carefully groomed older woman. She was caught by the fact that the woman's hands twisted nervously as she stood waiting.

Obeying an impulse Lia addressed her. "My, but that's a lovely suit you're wearing. It really makes you look very beautiful!"

The woman smiled hesitantly, thanking Lia. The bus came and they parted.

About a month later Lia stood on the same corner, again waiting for a bus. The same woman was there, but this time Lia noticed a different air about her. She bore herself with confidence and a look of self-assurance. When the woman saw Lia she smiled openly and came over to take her hand.

"I'm so glad to have this chance to see you again," she said warmly. "I've been wishing that I could thank you for what you did for me a month ago when you told me how nice I looked."

The woman went on to say that she had been recently widowed, and on that morning a month ago she had ventured out for the first time since her husband's death to look for a job. Lia's words were just what she needed to give her the necessary confidence to tackle employment agencies. That day she had found a very fine position, just what she needed for financial independence.

Of course moving from dependence to wholeness is never an easy matter. Just observe how this movement on the part of a child places stress on the relationship of child and parent! Letting go of those for whom we have once been completely responsible is foreign to the nature of persons with a high level of concern for others. Parents are usually concerned people and often tend to keep their children dependent on them long after that is warranted by the growth of the child. Unless they let go at the appropriate time, the growing child may fail to develop the feelings of autonomy which form the basis for living successfully as an adult.

In order to accomplish this there must be a willingness to let go of control on the part of the one and a willingness to be set free from protective custody on the part of the other, and both parties need to work at helping the other overcome the fears which come with change and newness and growing up.

On the mountain I learned that contradictory feelings fight for supremacy even though the dependent person longs for the freedom from anxiety—the *shalom*—which independence brings. The comfort of having someone else care for one, the security of living in a cocoon—all of this fights with the longing to be in charge of one's own life with the help of God alone.

How exciting it was for me to step out on that plateau of independence to which the mountain of struggle and loneliness had brought me! Being forced to depend wholly on myself and the strengthening Spirit and to find out for myself that the promise of Jesus' continuing presence really holds, was a fantastic experience.

In my aloneness I learned a new dimension of discipleship. When we give up and yield to God all that we are and all to which we lay claim, he moves in to make up for our loss. Like the Son, we put all things under the Father's feet and he becomes all in all (1 Cor. 15:27-28). For the moment we need nothing else and no one else. He is sufficient.

Without the sense of inwardness that develops best in solitude, the Christian becomes a doer only, and the springs of renewal dry up. The inner life of faith is nourished as one focuses on the presence of the Spirit, and the Spirit in turn makes the words of promise come alive in personal praise and in power to witness.

The kind of solitude required for developing inner strength is difficult to come by in our urbanized and televised existence. Even the close-knit family can be a deterrent. For complete growth, times of aloneness must be balanced against togetherness.

Alone on the plane, in the apartment, in the car, I found myself more and more aware of the Spirit's presence, conscious in new ways of his power and direction for making decisions, for witnessing, and for enlightenment. I felt that God was trying to compensate for the absence of my family by being especially gracious in visiting me with his presence.

On the *shalom*-plateau I lived with praise as my constant companion. I recall many occasions on which I was moved to prayer by knowing that God's Spirit was with me in fulfillment of Jesus' promise.

Once a speaking engagement forced me to drive alone a distance of 250 miles to a retreat center. Fall colors tinted the hills in sharp contrast to the gray, surrealistic mists floating in the valleys. In the early morning hours few cars traveled the glistening roadway, and I felt the world to be inhabited by God and me alone. Conviction of his presence brings confidence and power to witness.

With the power came opportunity. Every speaking assignment brought a response in personal need from individuals; every plane trip became an encounter with the lives of other travelers. One was hastening to the bedside of a dying relative; another was aching with the pain of a dying marriage. A middle-aged pastor who was assigned the seat next to me confessed that he was losing his faith and longed for a sure word of testimony to the presence of God in what seemed to be a God-forsaken world. A Canadian teacher traveling out of Chicago confessed his concern for a runaway child and a depressed wife.

Out of my solitude-born sureness of the presence of God in my own life came power to bring reassurance and a word of witness to others.

On the plateau, then, there is rest from the struggle. *Shalom* graces the spirit and the landscape. The feeling is one of goodness and strength and wholeness. A reminder comes to all strugglers that "there remains a sabbath rest for the people of God; for whoever enters God's rest also ceases from his labors as God did from his" (Heb. 4:9-10).

But the summit beckons. Reluctantly we shoulder our equipment. The plateau has refreshed us; we take confidence in the renewed conviction that with the Spirit's help, we'll make it to the top.

We move on, a little surer of foot and a bit straighter of shoulder.

The path is no less rocky, the ascent no less steep, but the Presence has refreshed us. Out of our new-found sense of individual wholeness we are better able to help each other, and we marvel at the new dimension of corporate wholeness which is ours.

Now we have worked out the problem of our physical separation. We decided to be together. Out of my own *shalom* I made the conscious decision to leave my job and join Erling in that warm climate where he is physically more comfortable now. Some regret attended that decision since so many good learnings and rewarding contacts came with the job.

But our *shalom* is only complete when we are together.

We wanted that to happen while we were still living and so took the steps necessary to end our separation.

When death comes, as it will to all of us, we will endure the separation, waiting for that final *shalom* when the resurrected life unites us with each other and the waiting Jesus.

Shalom.

The
Summit

ERLING:

The artist Blake portrays all humanity as a person standing with one foot on the lowest rung of a soaring ladder, looking up longingly to cry "I want! I want!"

Life appears to be mostly a bundle of wants. We want happiness; we want fulfillment; we want intimacy. We want some values we feel are important. We want to live significantly, vitally, as free, buoyant winners. But the question of the summit, the ultimate, takes center stage. Nothing shadows our lives more seriously than the hauntingly disturbing thought of our dying. The question of the end overhangs every detail of life. We know the struggle up the lonely mountain has only minor significance if we're not fully aware of the goal.

Nothing describes the source of the carefree, anxiety-less freedom of Jesus more than that remarkable phrase that sets the tone for his entire ministry of support to others: Jesus, "knowing that . . . he came *from* God and was going *to* God," took a towel and began washing his disciples' feet (John 13:3-5). His captivating poise, comforting calm, and fascinating singleness of purpose grew out of his clear understanding of his source and his destination. He encapsulated the conviction that no heart is pure that isn't passionately dedicated to an ultimate goal. Jesus' heart was set on his ultimate goal. He discovered a transparent joy on the climb as he endured the cross, said "No" to the pain, and earned his right to give his ultimate gift of heaven to all who dare to follow him.

We dare to follow him on that swaying bridge. The journey must begin just like his: knowing my source and my destination. These are my absolutes. My journey towards my summit of hope begins when I recognize that I have come from God. He initiated the invasion of my life. He first loved me and paid his Son's life for my soul. An awesome sense of security floods us when we realize this.

I remember vividly walking across a gorge some distance north of Tokyo. I was enroute to speak to students from the universities of that capital city. I rode four buses up the winding way to the mountain retreat. At the end of the road a giant chasm still separated me from my destination. The only way across was a rope bridge suspended threateningly in mid-air over the raging stream far below. Airy, dangerous—yet exciting!

I felt a rush of exhilaration as I stepped onto the swaying, jostling, bucking span. Before I gave my life to it, I checked the supports for the frail contrivance at the end where I was to begin my walk. I wanted to be sure they were secure before I trusted myself to its promise of safe passage. I still stepped out in faith, hoping that the supports on the other side were equally strong. There was security only in knowing that the same hands that had fashioned the supports on my end had designed them with equal care on the other end.

Because the bridge qualified at its starting point, I had hope that it would hold me at the finish.

This fact was never more dramatically illustrated for me than it was in the person of a young freckle-faced sixteen-year-old girl from California. I first saw her in Tokyo one night during the Olympic swim meet. My vantage point in the second row proved an ideal place to view the tense action in the gigantic pool as I focused on that young woman. That night she brought the giant crowd to its feet by fighting her way to a gold medal in the breast stroke. Television cameras cascaded pictures of the event all over the world. I was caught up in the excitement of knowing that this young neighbor of mine from faraway California had struggled to victory. My feelings went into orbit as I shouted my lungs out in moving appreciation.

Six months later I met her at a downtown Los Angeles gathering. Having her ear for a moment I said, "Winning that first gold medal must have been the most moving experience of your life." Quickly she countered, "Oh, no! That's not so!" Surprised, I pressed her, "What could be more exciting?"

Her answer came clearly, "The most exciting moment came for me when I *qualified* for the team."

Strenuous struggle earned her that right. The cost to qualify was the dedication of her life: eight hours daily practice, running miles, pulling wall weights. The disciplined life of a swimmer was her passion.

We remember a far more remarkable "qualifier" about whom St. Paul writes in his Colossian letter—the God "who has qualified us to share in the inheritance of the saints in light." Here he captures the glory of God's grace, that I am permitted to enter the race as a gift. My Lord has qualified for me. The excitement of being permitted to compete, the glad joy of sharing the struggle to the summit, the privilege of fighting to attain the ultimate goal, all have been a gift. His qualifications are available to me. I accept my inheritance. "As many as received him, to them gave he the right to become children of God" (John 1:12).

We check the initial support. We venture out on it and discover that it holds.

We've been permitted to join the illustrious company of Abraham and Sarah, Deborah and Samson, Priscilla and Acquila, Luther and Katherine, Susanna and Charles Wesley. All of us have accepted a purchased permission. "Come, for all things are ready." With them I entered life when I was baptized. This promised gift of God gave me rights and privileges, a priestly calling and a royal stance, a family and a future, a responsibility and a joy in doing it, and a living hope!

A perpetual exhilaration grips when we hang on to the fact that the supports on that end are anchored deep in a giant cross. It will hold because God planted that support, being pleased for some unbelievably wonderful reason to bruise his own Son for our sakes.

Heaven—that place where my Savior waits—is my ultimate home, but we experience it all along the way.

Many years ago the entire "heroes and heroines of faith" chapter in Hebrews had taken on new dimensions and meanings for us. In that 11th chapter we had met daring Noah again who "being warned by God concerning events as yet unseen, took heed and constructed an ark to save his own family"; quiet Sarah who permitted a miracle to happen because she "considered him faithful who promised"; a revolutionary Moses who endured illtreatment, a King's anger, and abuse because he "saw the one who cannot be seen!"

But the verse that really captures heaven right here and now is Hebrews 11:1. "Now faith is the substance of things hoped for, *the conviction of things not seen.*" When I risk believing, the invisible world begins to give me flash glimpses of its reality.

Like Boris Pasternak, the great Russian novelist. Enforced horrors in his homeland nearly shattered him. When worldwide fame scattered his cries for freedom beyond the borders of his country, life was made into a hell for him. His secret of endurance was simple.

"I couldn't have made it but for Jesus, the Christ," he said. *"He came to me."*

He came to me. That phrase pulses in my soul, and sings a duet with the same reality in my heart. Jesus not only empowers me with a future hope in the words, "I will come again to receive you to myself," but he comes again and again to reveal himself in the here and now. "I will come to you . . . I will not leave you an orphan

. . . Even in the valley of the shadow of death, I am with you."

The summit is secure because of what I experience now. "He that lives and believes in me has already passed from death to life."

Attuned to his presence, I am gripped by exhilaration whenever I feel the faint rustling of his seamless garment at my side. What a glad wonder—to know that I have a Presence, above me, around me, about me, behind me.

I sensed that Presence talking to a woman named Beth. Her outer world had literally caved in. Married at thirty to her "dream man," she lost him only a few weeks later when he was killed in an auto accident near the beach where I had broken my neck. Physically incapacitated with multiple sclerosis, she still glows with the kind of glory that Jesus shares with a receptive human.

Close to the summit of her mountain, she exercises her ministry on that last swaying bridge. Enthusiasm gives vibrancy to her voice when she describes her life. Supported by an academic pension and accredited as a professional counselor, she works avidly with young people crippled by drugs, with unmarried mothers, with unhappy married folk. Part of her limited funds are used to buy books she thinks helpful for her counselees. Threat and tension on her bridge cannot thwart her. Although she longs for her future reward in the presence of her Lord, it's very obvious that he's real to her now.

The viewpoints along the way up the mountain all have their own claim to beauty, but the closer one gets to the summit the more breathtaking each panorama becomes. The higher one gets, the greater the danger, but the more vivid is his Presence.

The setting was an ominous and danger-filled one when I stood in the pulpit of a mortuary one day before a group of 150 cyclists. They were members of three "chopper gangs" who had come to pay their last respects to one of their own who had been cut down by a shotgun blast on the freeway offramp.

His parents told me nothing about their son's involvement with these destructive gangs when they called me for the service. When I talked to them about their son's life, they failed to mention that he was the seventh "see-saw" victim of gang warfare.

So there they sat—a tightly disciplined crowd, silently remote, leather clad and seemingly unwashed. Some had quiet little teen-age girls beside them, on their backs leather name pads with such inscriptions as, "Julie, property of Jim." Interspersed among them were 50 plain-clothes policemen. Dozens of other police officers were outside in vans, on cycles, and on foot, recording licenses, taking pictures, making notes.

I did what I could that day to make Jesus come alive for them. I pleaded with them to stop the pointless killings, arguing that retribution only plants seeds for continuing death on both sides. I pointed them to Jesus whose love overcame any bitterness he might have harbored for those who nailed him to the cross and brought words of pardon to his lips.

When the service ended, everyone left except the gang members, one mortician and myself. Five intensely quiet minutes went by as I stood next to the casket. The tensions grew as no one moved.

At last one who was apparently a leader arose. Clad in a cutaway leather vest, dirty dungarees and boots, he moved slowly toward the casket. When only six feet from the body of his former colleague, he deliberately unrolled a leather insignia taken from the jacket of the sixth victim who had been slain by their own group. Cooly contemptuous, he tossed the foot-square coat of arms on the floor immediately below the body. With visible malice he walked on it as he stepped forward to salute his former gang member.

Soon the others followed. Some walked on the emblem, some scrubbed their feet on it, some cleared their throats and spat on it.

But then came the moment from eternity. I thought of Paul when he addressed the sophisticated Athenians on Mars Hill. Some called him an "ignorant show-off," some debated academically with him, some thought him an unveiler of "strange gods" as he talked about the resurrection of Jesus. But "some men joined him and believed; among them was Dionysus . . . a woman named Damaris, and some others" (Acts 17:16ff.).

Before me one of the strange group filing by paused and looked at me. Then he made the sign of a circle with his fingers, as though in witness to a newly formed commitment. With deliberate care he avoided stepping on the emblem on the floor. He joined me on the swaying bridge anchored in a Cross. I was aware of the danger he was courting; but I was also aware of the Presence.

On the swaying bridge between two eternities the calling is to servanthood and witness. On the way to the summit there's much to be done. In the foot-washing Christ there's a whole new model for serving, and when we care to move out in ministry with him, we discover a glad exuberance.

There's security: "Nothing can separate me from the love of God in Christ Jesus my Lord."

There's challenge: "Take up your cross, which is your ministry of suffering and caring for my sake and the gospel's."

There's a potential: "All things are possible to him who believes."

There are endless resources: "My God, with all his abundant wealth, in Christ Jesus, will supply all of your needs."

When I dare believe what he tells me, he responds through endless happenings to make his Presence visible.

As we move on toward the summit and the culmination of our climb, we become increasingly sensitive to the beauty around us: the wonder in a child's eyes, the touch of a friend's hand, the glorious variety in all of God's family on earth, the music of many languages. My entire world, backdrop for God's redemptive work, comes alive with beauty.

A certain anguish fills us also as we approach the end of the journey. Behind us lie the broken promises, the unfulfilled commitments, the neighbors we were too blind to see. We weep for ourselves and for a world that may be very little better because we walked its paths. Wars are still fought, children still starve, people are still exploited by other people. There are no excuses; we have not done all that we could have done.

But the summit is not yet here. The important thing now is to be sensitive to the path yet ahead. There are still people and there is still the Presence. Like Jesus who saw his destination not far ahead in the shape of the waiting Cross, we still take up a towel and serve.

But the intensity of anticipation increases as we fix our hope on the final summit. We stand on tiptoe with Peter when he rejoices: "Blessed be the God and Father of our Lord Jesus Christ! By his great mercy we have been born anew to a living hope through the resurrection of Jesus Christ from the dead, and to an inheritance which is imperishable, undefiled, and unfading, kept in heaven for you, who by God's power are guarded through faith for a salvation ready to be revealed in the last time. In this you rejoice, though now for a little while you may have to suffer various trials, so that the genuineness of your faith, more precious than gold which though perishable is tested by fire, may redound to praise and glory and honor at the revelation Jesus Christ" (1 Peter 1:3-7).

Now our experience is like that of a neighbor who accepted a special invitation to attend the coronation of the Queen of England. Years later her eyes still sparkled when she unveiled for us the excitement she experienced in being permitted into the hall just outside the Coronation Room. With eyes wide open her whole being responded as she shared through that open door and flung-wide windows the sights, sounds, sensations, and the aromas of that significant event. She could share all of its intensity although she still hadn't "entered in."

Some day we shall enter in; we are designed, redeemed, and marked for the summit. Jesus has promised that he will be waiting for that reunion, the bread and the wine of his presence ready for the celebration.

We have endured; his Spirit has enabled us to keep on keeping on. We have united with other climbers to rescue each other from the abyss of despair. The mountain is behind us.

Thank God for the mountain!